BABY

by Linda Spivey

A Gift of Memories

havoc
PUBLISHING

©1998 Havoc Publishing

ISBN 1-57977-121-1

Published and created by Havoc Publishing

San Diego, California

First Printing, January 1998

Made in China

Design © 1997 Linda Spivey
Under License from Penny Lane Publishing, Inc.

Please write to us for more information on our

Havoc Publishing Record Books and Products.

HAVOC PUBLISHING

6330 Nancy Ridge Drive, Suite 104

San Diego, California 92121

For:

_____

You are our special gift
from the Lord

This book of cherished
memories is kept for you by
your Mother with Love.

CONTENTS

Your Mother

Your Father

How We Met

Family Tree

Family History

Your Father's Heritage

Your Mother's Heritage

Aunts and Uncles

Birth Announcement

Family Photographs

The News of Your Arrival

Ultra-Sound Photographs

Preparation

Showers

The Day you were Born

Special Features

Your first Visitors

Birth Certificate

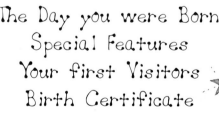

CONTENTS

Hand Prints and Foot Prints
World Events
Local News
Popular Personalities
The Early Days
Milestones
Your Favorite Things
Photographs
God Loved You Too
Your Caregivers
Your Future
Doctor Visits
Immunizations
Growth Chart
Smiles
Your First Home
Your First Birthday
Photographs
Christmas Traditions

Your father and I Love you very much and we want you to know this about us:

~ Mother ~

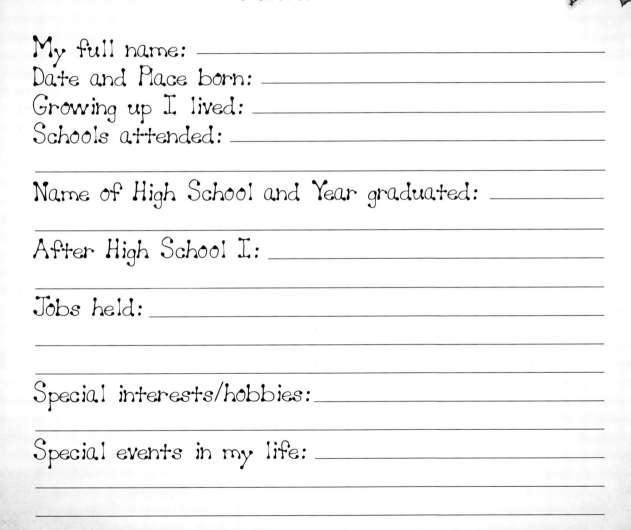

My full name: _____

Date and Place born: _____

Growing up I lived: _____

Schools attended: _____

_____

Name of High School and Year graduated: _____

_____

After High School I: _____

_____

Jobs held: _____

_____

_____

Special interests/hobbies: _____

_____

Special events in my life: _____

_____

_____

~ Father ~

His full name: _____

Date and Place born: _____

Growing up he lived: _____

Schools attended: _____

_____

Name of High School and Year graduated: _____

_____

After High School he: _____

_____

Jobs held: _____

_____

_____

_____

_____

_____

Special interests/hobbies: _____

_____

Special events in his life: _____

_____

_____

This is how we met: _____
_____
_____
_____

When we met I was ____ years old, and your father _____
We were married on _____ by: _____
This is about Our Wedding day: _____
_____
_____
_____

When you were born I was ____ years old, your father was _____

Photo of

Mother

Photo of

Father

Great Grandmother's/Fathers

Grand Father

Grandmother

Mother

Great Grandmother's/Father's

Grandfather

Grandmother

Father

My
Family
Tree

Date I was Born

Weight and length

Where I was Born

MY NAME

MY Brother's/Sisters

hSpivey©

Mother's Parents were married; date and place: _____

_____

When they were married Grandmother was ___ years old
and Grandfather was ___ years old.
Their first home was: _____

_____

_____

Any special thoughts: _____

_____

_____

Father's Parents were married; date and place: _____

_____

When they were married Grandmother was ___ years old
and Grandfather was ___ years old.
Their first home was: _____

_____

_____

Any special thoughts: _____

_____

_____

Your Family Tree
Your Grandmother ~ Father's Side

Grandmother's full name: _____

Date and Place Born: _____

Growing up she lived: _____

Schools attended: _____
_____

Jobs held: _____
_____

Special interests: _____
_____
_____

Interesting facts about her: _____
_____
_____
_____

Brothers and Sisters: _____
_____

Your Family Tree
Your Grandfather ~ Father's Side

Grandfather's full name: _____

Date and Place Born: _____

Growing up he lived: _____

Schools attended: _____

_____

Jobs held: _____

_____

Special interests: _____

_____

_____

Interesting facts about him: _____

_____

_____

_____

Brothers and Sisters: _____

_____

Your Family Tree
Your Grandmother ~ Mother's Side

Grandmother's full name: _____

Date and Place Born: _____

Growing up she lived: _____

Schools attended: _____

_____

Jobs held: _____

_____

Special interests: _____

_____

_____

Interesting facts about her: _____

_____

_____

_____

Brothers and Sisters: _____

_____

Your Family Tree
Your Grandfather ~ Mother's Side

Grandfather's full name: _____

Date and Place Born: _____

Growing up he lived: _____

Schools attended: _____

_____

Jobs held: _____

_____

Special interests: _____

_____

_____

Interesting facts about him: _____

_____

_____

_____

Brothers and Sisters: _____

_____

Your Aunts and Uncles on My side of the family are: _____

_____

_____

_____

_____

_____

_____

_____

_____

_____

Your Aunts and Uncles on Your Father's side are: _____

_____

_____

_____

_____

_____

_____

_____

_____

_____

 ~ Our Birth Announcement ~

 ~ Hospital Bracelets ~

Family Photographs

Father unto thee, I Pray
Watch over me, Night and Day

As I Sleep and As I Play
Guide Me in Your
Loving Way

Baby's Room

L. Spivey ©

When I learned you were on the way my first
reaction was: _____
_____
_____

Father's reaction: _____
_____
_____

The first people we told were: _____
_____

Pre-natal visits were to Dr. _____
Your due date was set at: _____
Pre-natal tests done: _____
_____
_____

This is how the pregnancy went: _____
_____
_____
_____
_____
_____

Place Ultra-sound photographs here: Date done: _____

The first time I felt you kick was: _____

_____

_____

_____

_____

_____

_____

This is what we did to prepare for you. (Books read, classes taken, advice taken from): _____

_____

_____

_____

_____

_____

_____

_____

What we did to prepare your room: _____

_____

_____

_____

_____

_____

_____

_____

_____

Special Events
for you   ♥ ♥ ♥ ♥   You were showered
                                   with many gifts

Shower event: Time ~ Place ~ activities ~ special thoughts

_____

_____

_____

_____

_____

_____

_____

_____

_____

_____

_____

Shower Gifts

Friends and Family   Gift Given

The day you were born was very special. Here is the story of our labor and delivery: _____

What a beautiful child. Your hair color: _____

Your eyes: _____ Any birthmarks? _____

You look like: _____

_____

We named You: _____

_____

We gave You this name because: _____

_____

_____

Other names we considered ~ Both Boy and Girl:

_____

_____

Nicknames we have for you: _____

_____

_____

Your first Visitors
(comments please)

A B C

Welcome

BABY

Name:
Born: Time:
Weight: Length:
Proud Parents

hSpivey©

~ Welcome Baby ~

Birth Certificate

~ Hand Print ~

~ Foot Print ~

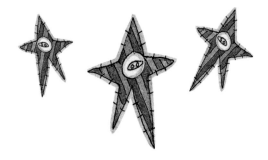

Here is what was happening the day and the
year that you were born . . . World Events:

(Attach headlines from newspapers or fill in information)

Local News: (Save newspaper of Birth Announcement)

What things cost the year you were born:

A gallon of milk: _____

A loaf of bread: _____

A pizza: _____

A Hamburger out: _____

A gallon of Gasoline: _____

A newspaper: _____

1st class postage _____

<table>
<tr><td>place
postage
stamp
here</td></tr>
</table>

Popular Personalities

Music: _____

T.V.: _____

Movies: _____

Sports: _____

Other: _____

Your Parents Favorites

Music: _____

T.V.: _____

Movies: _____

Sports: _____

Fashion trends today: _____

_____

_____

World Leaders: _____

_____

_____

_____

The early days after birth you slept . . . _____

_____

_____

_____

I fed you: _____

_____

When you were awake you: _____

_____

_____

_____

Picture of Baby sleeping

Milestones

The first time you slept through the night: _____

My thoughts about this: _____

_____

_____

Turned over: _____

Sits alone: _____

Holds a toy: _____

First smile: _____ Laughed: _____

First solid food was: _____ on: _____

You drank from a cup first on: _____

Crawls: _____

Stands up: _____

First steps hanging on: _____

First steps alone: _____ with: _____

Your first words were: _____

_____

Your first kiss given on: _____ to: _____

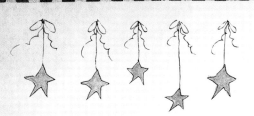 # Milestones

Your first tub bath: _____

Your first public appearance: _____

_____

_____

Your first hair cut was given on: _____

by: _____

Photo   Photo

Before   after

Haircut   Haircut

☆ Lock of hair ☆

As you grew you had likes and dislikes. Here are a few
of your favorite things:

at six months   ★   at one year   ★   at second year

Favorite Story Book: _____

Song: _____

Favorite game: _____

Favorite toy: _____

Outfit/and where it came from: _____

_____

Favorite foods at home and eating out: _____

_____

_____

Your favorite color: _____

Your best friend: _____

Favorite T.V. show: _____

_____

There were some things you definitely didn't like ~ they were

_____

hSpivey ©

~ Photographs ~

Humpty-Dumpty sat on a wall, Humpty-Dumpty had a great fall.

Pat-a-cake, Pat-a-cake baker's man, bake me a cake as fast as you can.

Mary, Mary, quite contrary, How does your garden grow?

Rock-a-bye baby, on the tree top, when the wind blows the cradle will rock.

hSpivey ©

~ Photographs ~

Pat-a-cake, Pat-a-cake bakers man, bake me a cake as fast as you can.

Mary, Mary, quite contrary, How does your garden grow?

Rock-a-bye baby, on the tree top, when the wind blows the cradle will rock.

hSpivey ©

God Loves You Too

Your Baptism/Dedication/Ceremony was held on: _____

at: _____

Performed by: _____

Family and Friends Present: _____

_____

_____

Photos of this
special event

Your First experiences in church were:

_____

_____

_____

_____

_____

_____

_____

First prayers learned: _____

_____

_____

_____

_____

Your Friends at church were: _____

_____

_____

_____

_____

Your Caregivers

Your father and I couldn't be with you always. Your very
favorite babysitter was: _____

_____

_____

_____

Special activities you attended: _____

_____

_____

_____

Neighbors and friends you played with: _____

_____

_____

_____

_____

_____

Special Places you visited:_____

_____

_____

_____

_____

the Lord, "Plans to Prosper you and not to harm you

Plans to give you hope and a future." Jeremiah 29: 11-12

"For I know the Plans I have for you, declares)

Call upon me, come to me, Pray to me and I will listen

Plans
Prayers
Promises
Blessings

Plans
Prayers
Promises
Blessings

~ Your Future ~

Our Plans and Prayers for you: _____

_____

_____

_____

_____

_____

_____

_____

_____

_____

_____

_____

hSpivey©

An Apple a Day Keeps the Doctor Away
An Ounce of Prevention is Better than a Pound of Cure
Love and Laughter are the best medicine
God Heals and the Doctor takes the Fee
THE DOCTOR IS IN
E
N Z
Y L B
NURSE KIT
LSpivey ©

We visited the Doctor to keep you healthy, but sometimes you got sick. Your Pediatrician was Dr. _____
Record of visits to the Doctor:

Date   Reason for visit
_____

_____

_____

_____

_____

_____

_____

_____

_____

_____

_____

_____

_____

_____

Immunizations

	Date given	Reaction
HIB Haemophilus:		

Hepatitis B:

Allergies:

Immunizations

Date given   Reaction

DPT (Diphtheria Tetanus Pertussis):

_____

_____

_____

_____

OPV (Oral Polio Vaccine): _____

_____

_____

_____

_____

MMR (Measles Mumps Rubella): _____

_____

Growth Chart

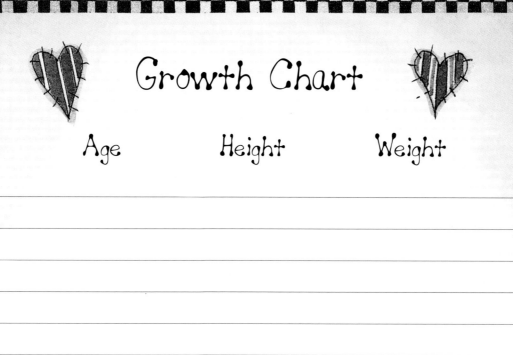

Date	Age	Height	Weight

Smiles

Your first tooth appeared: _____

Your first visit to the dentist was on: _____

to see Dr._____ You were ____ years old.

Your age when tooth first appeared: _____

	Upper	Right	Left
1.	Central Incisor		
2.	Lateral Incisor		
3.	Cuspid		
4.	First molar		
5.	Second molar		

Left   Right

Upper

Lower

	Lower	Right	Left
1.	Central Incisor		
2.	Lateral Incisor		
3.	Cuspid		
4.	First molar		
5.	Second molar		

Your first tooth lost was: _____

~ Your First Home ~

Address: _____

_____

Thoughts about this Home: _____

_____

_____

_____

_____

_____

Photograph of Home

~ Your First Birthday ~

It's hard to believe you're already one year old. Here is how we celebrated: _____

_____

_____

_____

_____

Gifts you received/and from who: _____

_____

_____

_____

_____

Special Thoughts: _____

_____

_____

_____

1st year Photo

1ST

~ Photographs ~

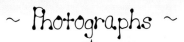

~ Photographs ~

FrEE BEAR Hugs

Wishing You the Blessings of CHRISTMAS

merry Christmas

S.Spivey©

⭐ Christmas Traditions ⭐

Your first Christmas we: _____

_____

_____

_____

_____

_____

_____

This is how your family celebrates Christmas: _____

_____

_____

_____

_____

_____

_____

_____

_____

_____

_____

Available Record Books From Havoc

Baby	Mothers & Daughters
Coach	My Pregnancy
College Life	Our Honeymoon
Couples	Retirement
Dad	School Days
Girlfriends	Single Life
Golf	Sisters
Grandmother	Teacher
Grandparents	Traveling Adventures
Mom	Tying the Knot

havoc
PUBLISHING